STUDY GUIDE

TRACTION

Published by AVAIL

ISBN: 978-1-962401-13-5   1 2 3 4 5 6 7 8 9 10

Printed in the United States of America

TRACTION

FIVE PROVEN PRINCIPLES FOR UNSTOPPABLE GROWTH

CHRIS SONKSEN

AVAIL

CONTENTS

Chapter 1. Get on Board...6

Chapter 2. Engine: Growth Strategies..................................... 10

Chapter 3. Fuel: Leadership and Finances 16

Chapter 4. Tracks: Staying on Course 22

Chapter 5. Conductor: The Essential Role of the Pastor..... 28

Chapter 6. Cars: Alignment of Staff, Leaders,
             and the Congregation 34

Chapter 7. From Wood-Fired to Bullet Trains...................... 40

TRACTION

FIVE PROVEN PRINCIPLES FOR UNSTOPPABLE GROWTH

CHRIS SONKSEN

GET ON BOARD

Momentum works for churches of any size.

READING
TIME

As you read
Chapter 1:
"Get on Board"
in *Traction*,
review, reflect
on, and respond
to the text by
answering
the following
questions.

REVIEW, REFLECT, AND RESPOND

In your role as a Christian church leader, can you identify a specific instance or period when you felt the ministry or church was stuck? What factors contributed to this stagnation?

_____

_____

_____

_____

_____

_____

_____

_____

_____

Considering the challenges of generating momentum, how have you involved and empowered your church leadership team or congregation in the process? Share examples of collaborative efforts that have successfully moved your church forward.

_____

_____

_____

_____

_____

_____

_____

_____

_____

Reflecting on the past year, share specific strategies or initiatives you implemented to break through inertia and generate momentum within your church community. What were the successful outcomes, and what challenges did you encounter?

_____

_____

_____

_____

_____

_____

_____

_____

_____

_____

_____

_____

_____

_____

Going deeper into the concept of feeling stuck, what do you believe are the root issues that often hinder progress? How can you address or overcome these issues to foster momentum? As you read the brief descriptions of the train metaphor's components, which one(s) do you need to work on? What difference will it make?

_____

_____

_____

_____

_____

_____

_____

_____

_____

_____

_____

_____

_____

_____

As you contemplate the changes or improvements you need to make based on the train metaphor, consider the long-term impact on your church community. How do you envision these adjustments contributing to the overall mission and vision of your church?

_____

_____

_____

_____

_____

_____

_____

_____

_____

_____

_____

_____

_____

ENGINE:
GROWTH STRATEGIES

A train with a broken-down engine doesn't make any progress, and one that's barely moving doesn't have the power to climb hills or get past obstacles.

READING TIME

As you read Chapter 2: "Engine: Growth Strategies" in *Traction*, review, reflect on, and respond to the text by answering the following questions.

REVIEW, REFLECT, AND RESPOND

Reflect on your position on the continuum of trusting God completely versus relying on strategic planning. How has your perspective evolved over time, and how does it influence your decision-making as a Christian leader?

_____

_____

_____

_____

_____

_____

_____

If you were to ask your staff and board members about your approach to trusting God versus depending on strategies, what do you think their responses would be? How might their perceptions align or differ from your self-assessment?

_____

_____

_____

_____

_____

_____

_____

_____

_____

Have you ever identified with rebel staff members who express frustration or a sense of stagnation within the church? Share instances where you may have resonated with their perspectives and discuss how these experiences influenced your leadership.

_____

_____

_____

_____

_____

_____

Share specific instances where you felt the church was stuck, similar to the experiences mentioned in this chapter. How did you navigate these challenges, and what strategies did you employ to break through the sense of stagnation?

_____

_____

_____

_____

_____

_____

As you read about growth strategies in chapter 2, which specific strategies resonate with you and align with the vision of your church? How do you plan to incorporate or adapt these strategies to foster growth within your congregation?

_____

_____

_____

_____

_____

_____

_____

Considering the growth strategies discussed in the chapter, how do
you plan to implement these strategies in your ministry context?
What adjustments or customizations will be necessary to ensure
they align with the unique needs and culture of your congregation?
Be specific.

_____

_____

_____

_____

_____

_____

Describe how each of the exercises in this chapter could help you:

The 90-Day Run:

_____

_____

_____

_____

The 90-Day Window:

_____

_____

_____

_____

Boxes and Batons:

_____

_____

_____

_____

_____

Riverbanks:

_____

_____

_____

_____

_____

Creating an Invite Culture:

_____

_____

_____

_____

_____

Evaluate: Which ones do you need to prioritize?

_____

_____

_____

_____

_____

_____

Educate: How will you explain the concepts to your team and your board?

_____

_____

_____

_____

_____

_____

_____

_____

Establish: What are the first steps you need to take?

_____

_____

_____

_____

_____

_____

_____

Execute: When and how will you implement it (or them)?

_____

_____

_____

_____

_____

_____

_____

FUEL: LEADERSHIP AND FINANCES

Trains have morphed over the years to use more powerful and efficient fuels, but in churches, the fuel remains the same: it's all about the valuable resources of leaders and money.

READING TIME

As you read Chapter 3: "Fuel: Leadership and Finances" in *Traction*, review, reflect on, and respond to the text by answering the following questions.

REVIEW, REFLECT, AND RESPOND

Reflect on pastors you know who are facing shortages in both leaders and finances. How has this deficit impacted their personal lives and the overall effectiveness of their ministries? Have you ever faced a shortage in these areas? Discuss potential strategies to address these challenges.

_____

_____

_____

_____

_____

_____

_____

_____

_____

_____

_____

_____

_____

_____

_____

_____

_____

_____

_____

_____

_____

Identify pastors who have sufficient leaders and financial resources. What distinguishes them, their teams, and their churches from those facing deficits? Explore the key factors contributing to their success and consider how these insights can be applied in your ministry.

_____

_____

_____

_____

_____

_____

_____

_____

_____

Within your church, identify individuals holding leadership titles but primarily functioning as managers. What potential consequences might arise from this discrepancy, and how can you address or redirect their roles to align with effective leadership principles?

_____

_____

_____

_____

_____

_____

_____

_____

Recognize individuals in your church who demonstrate the potential to become influential leaders. How can you provide them with more attention, mentorship, and opportunities to nurture their leadership skills? Share specific plans for investing in these rising stars.

_____

_____

_____

_____

_____

_____

_____

_____

_____

_____

Consider the idea of investing time in leadership circles. Do you believe it would be time well spent? Why or why not? Discuss the potential benefits of participating in leadership circles, including networking, learning opportunities, and collaborative problem-solving.

_____

_____

_____

_____

_____

_____

_____

_____

_____

Based on the insights from chapter 3, what specific strategies can you implement in your ministry to address leadership and financial challenges? How can you create a culture that fosters both effective leadership development and sound financial stewardship?

_____

_____

_____

_____

_____

_____

_____

_____

_____

As a Christian leader, how do you balance the dual responsibilities of effective leadership and sound financial management? Share experiences where finding this balance was challenging and discuss strategies for maintaining equilibrium in both areas.

_____

_____

_____

_____

_____

_____

_____

_____

_____

Evaluate: Which of the exercises related to money look most attractive to you?

_____

_____

_____

_____

_____

_____

Educate: Explain how you would use them and what difference they would make.

_____

_____

_____

_____

_____

Establish: What are your first steps of implementation?

_____

_____

_____

_____

Execute: When and how will you take those steps?

_____

_____

_____

_____

TRACKS: STAYING ON COURSE

Hard work is commendable, but wise work is far better than pushing yourself to the point of burnout.

READING TIME

As you read
Chapter 4:
"Tracks: Staying
on Course"
in *Traction*,
review, reflect
on, and respond
to the text by
answering
the following
questions.

REVIEW, REFLECT, AND RESPOND

Articulate your church's mission statement.
How well is it known and understood within
your congregation? Discuss how the mission
statement aligns with the overall purpose
and calling of your church.

_____

_____

_____

_____

_____

_____

_____

_____

_____

_____

_____

_____

_____

_____

_____

_____

_____

_____

_____

_____

_____

_____

_____

_____

Share your church's vision statement and discuss its clarity and impact. How does the vision statement inspire and guide the congregation? In what ways is the vision communicated and embraced within the church community?

_____

_____

_____

_____

_____

_____

_____

_____

_____

_____

Evaluate the strategies currently in place within your church. Which ones are proving to be particularly effective in advancing the mission and vision? Discuss specific examples and the positive outcomes associated with these strategies.

_____

_____

_____

_____

_____

_____

_____

_____

_____

_____

Reflect on your church's values. How would you categorize them into core, aspirational, and accidental values? Discuss the importance of each category and explore ways to reinforce and align the values with the overall mission and vision.

_____

_____

_____

_____

_____

_____

_____

_____

_____

_____

As the pastor, how do you actively communicate and reinforce the church's mission, vision, and values? Share specific methods and examples of how you engage the congregation in understanding and embracing these foundational elements.

_____

_____

_____

_____

_____

_____

_____

_____

_____

_____

In times of decision-making or change, how do you ensure that the decisions align with the core values of the church? Share experiences where maintaining consistency with core values played a crucial role in the leadership and direction of the church.

_____

_____

_____

_____

_____

_____

Given the dynamic nature of ministry, how do you respond to changes in strategies while staying true to the mission and vision? Share instances where strategic adjustments were necessary and discuss the process of ensuring alignment with the overall vision.

_____

_____

_____

_____

_____

_____

Evaluate: Which of the exercises in this chapter might work well for you and your team?

_____

_____

_____

_____

_____

_____

Educate: Who needs the exercises explained so they make a difference?

_____

_____

_____

_____

_____

_____

_____

Establish: What's your first step?

_____

_____

_____

_____

_____

_____

_____

Execute: How will you make real progress?

_____

_____

_____

_____

_____

_____

_____

CONDUCTOR: THE ESSENTIAL ROLE OF THE PASTOR

The conductor on a train isn't the engineer, but sometimes, the engineer needs to do some diagnostics with the conductor to see if he's functioning well.

READING TIME

As you read Chapter 5: "Conductor: The Essential Role of the Pastor" in *Traction*, review, reflect on, and respond to the text by answering the following questions.

REVIEW, REFLECT, AND RESPOND

Reflect on ways to distinguish whether a church or staff team is stuck due to a personal issue with the conductor or if there's a need for different strategies. What diagnostic tools or assessments could be useful in making this determination?

_____

_____

_____

_____

_____

_____

_____

_____

When dealing with individuals who may be fragile and defensive, what are some effective approaches to address these issues compassionately? How can you create a supportive environment for open communication and growth, even when individuals may not outwardly express fragility?

_____

_____

_____

_____

_____

_____

_____

Explore the potential benefits of implementing the "First Day Experience" exercise with your team, as discussed in the chapter. How might this exercise contribute to team dynamics and identify areas for improvement? Consider the likelihood of team members being honest and discuss strategies to foster transparency.

_____

_____

_____

_____

_____

_____

_____

_____

_____

Reflect on the honesty within your team dynamics. Do you believe your team members would be honest with you about their experiences and challenges? Why or why not? Discuss strategies for cultivating a culture of openness and trust within the team.

_____

_____

_____

_____

_____

_____

_____

_____

_____

_____

Following this chapter's insights, how would you describe the essential role of the conductor in the context of a church leader? Consider the responsibilities, qualities, and skills highlighted in the chapter and discuss how these align with your own understanding of the pastoral role.

_____

_____

_____

_____

_____

_____

_____

_____

_____

Share experiences where personal challenges with leadership affected the overall effectiveness of your church or team. How did you navigate these challenges, and what strategies were implemented to overcome obstacles to growth and progress?

_____

_____

_____

_____

_____

_____

_____

_____

_____

Discuss ways to create a culture within your team that encourages vulnerability and authenticity. How can leaders model vulnerability, and what practices can be implemented to foster an environment where team members feel comfortable addressing personal challenges and suggesting strategic changes?

_____

_____

_____

_____

_____

_____

Given the importance of the conductor's personal growth, what specific strategies can be employed to support the ongoing development of leadership skills, emotional intelligence, and self-awareness? How can these strategies contribute to the overall health of the team and the church?

_____

_____

_____

_____

_____

Evaluate: Which of the exercises in this chapter might work well for you and your team?

_____

_____

_____

_____

_____

_____

_____

Educate: Who needs the exercises explained so they make a difference?

_____

_____

_____

_____

_____

_____

Establish: What's your first step?

_____

_____

_____

_____

_____

_____

Execute: How will you make real progress?

_____

_____

_____

_____

_____

_____

CARS: ALIGNMENT OF STAFF, LEADERS, AND THE CONGREGATION

Countless little things, if they aren't noticed and addressed, can cause a train (or a church) to derail.

READING TIME

As you read Chapter 6: "Cars: Alignment of Staff, Leaders, and the Congregation" in *Traction*, review, reflect on, and respond to the text by answering the following questions.

REVIEW, REFLECT, AND RESPOND

Reflect on ways to identify when a team is not aligned with the vision and values of the church. What specific signs or behaviors might indicate a lack of alignment, and how can these be addressed proactively?

_____

_____

_____

_____

_____

_____

_____

Share your experiences with a team that was out of alignment with the vision and values. What challenges did you face, and how did it impact the church, the team, and your own leadership? Discuss the lessons learned and strategies employed to realign the team.

_____

_____

_____

_____

_____

_____

_____

_____

_____

Reflect on the consequences of a misaligned team in your past experience. How did it affect the church community, the dynamics within the team, and your own leadership effectiveness? Discuss the long-term impact and any measures taken to mitigate negative outcomes.

_____

_____

_____

_____

_____

_____

_____

_____

_____

Consider the statement, "Healthy churches cause unhealthy people to leave, but unhealthy churches cause healthy people to leave." Do you agree or disagree with this statement, and why? Share examples or observations that support your perspective and discuss the implications for church leadership.

_____

_____

_____

_____

_____

_____

_____

_____

_____

Explore the roles of honesty and humility in the process of bringing a team back into alignment. How can you foster a culture of open communication and humility within the team? Share experiences where honesty and humility played a crucial role in realigning the team with the church's vision and values.

_____

_____

_____

_____

_____

_____

_____

_____

_____

Based on the insights from this chapter, what specific strategies can be implemented to ensure alignment among staff, leaders, and the congregation? Discuss practical steps for cultivating a shared vision and values that resonate throughout the entire church community.

_____

_____

_____

_____

_____

_____

_____

_____

_____

_____

Discuss ways to build and sustain a culture of alignment within your church. How can you consistently reinforce the importance of shared values and vision? Share examples of initiatives or practices that contribute to a unified and aligned church community.

_____

_____

_____

_____

_____

_____

_____

_____

_____

_____

_____

Evaluate: Which of the exercises in this chapter might work well for you and your team?

_____

_____

_____

_____

_____

_____

_____

_____

_____

_____

_____

Educate: Who needs the exercises explained so they make a difference?

_____

_____

_____

_____

_____

_____

_____

Establish: What's your first step?

_____

_____

_____

_____

_____

_____

_____

Execute: How will you make real progress?

_____

_____

_____

_____

_____

_____

_____

FROM WOOD-FIRED TO BULLET TRAINS

God has called you, He has crafted you with talents and experience, and He has put you in the right place to accomplish His divine purposes.

READING TIME

As you read Chapter 7: "From Wood-Fired to Bullet Trains" in *Traction*, review, reflect on, and respond to the text by answering the following questions.

REVIEW, REFLECT, AND RESPOND

Reflect on the importance of seeing ourselves "in process" as we learn to lead and serve. Why is it crucial to acknowledge that leadership development is an ongoing journey rather than a destination? How does this perspective contribute to personal and professional growth?

_____

_____

_____

_____

_____

_____

_____

_____

_____

_____

_____

_____

_____

_____

_____

_____

_____

_____

_____

_____

Identify the most important lessons and tools you've gained from the book. How have these insights impacted your understanding of leadership and service in a Christian context? Share specific examples or concepts that resonated with you.

_____

_____

_____

_____

_____

_____

_____

_____

Discuss when and how you plan to use the lessons and tools acquired from this book in your leadership role. Are there specific situations or challenges within your ministry where these insights can be applied? Share practical strategies for incorporating these lessons into your leadership approach.

_____

_____

_____

_____

_____

_____

_____

_____

_____

_____

What will be your first step in implementing the lessons and tools discussed in this book? Share a specific action plan or timeline for incorporating these insights into your leadership practice. Discuss any potential challenges and how you plan to overcome them.

_____

_____

_____

_____

_____

_____

_____

_____

_____

In what ways has your understanding of leadership and service evolved as a result of reading this book? Reflect on your personal growth throughout the reading process and how it has shaped your perspective on Christian leadership.

_____

_____

_____

_____

_____

_____

_____

_____

How do the lessons and tools from this book align with the specific context of your ministry? Discuss ways in which these insights can be contextualized and applied to address the unique challenges and opportunities within your church community.

_____

_____

_____

_____

_____

_____

_____

_____

Consider how you can involve others in your ministry in the learning process from this book. Are there aspects of this book's teachings that can be shared with your leadership team, congregation, or other stakeholders? Discuss strategies for promoting a culture of continuous learning within your community.

_____

_____

_____

_____

_____

_____

_____

_____

Establish criteria or indicators to measure the impact of implementing this book's insights in your leadership role. How will you assess the effectiveness of these lessons in enhancing your leadership skills and the overall health of your ministry?

_____

_____

_____

_____

_____

_____

_____

_____

_____

Outline a plan for ongoing leadership development. What additional resources, training, or practices do you intend to explore to continue your growth as a Christian leader? Discuss the importance of continuous learning and improvement in the realm of ministry leadership.

_____

_____

_____

_____

_____

_____

_____

_____

_____

www.ingramcontent.com/pod-product-compliance
Lightning Source LLC
Chambersburg PA
CBHW070051100426
42734CB00040B/2983